GIANT DINOSAURS

THE BIGGEST REPTILES TO EVER WALK THE EARTH!

PAUL HARRISON

ARCTURUS

GIGANOTOSAURUS

When *Giganotosaurus* was first discovered in Argentina, it started a big debate—was this dinosaur the biggest meat-eater ever?

Biggest of all

Many paleontologists believe that *Giganotosaurus* was the largest of all the dinosaur carnivores—even larger than *Tyrannosaurus rex*. From findings made so far, it certainly seemed to be longer and taller than its more famous rival. However, like *Carcharodontosaurus*, it also seemed to be more lightly built than *Tyrannosaurus rex*, so the argument continues about who was the king of the meat-eaters.

TRIASSIC	JURASSIC	CRETACEOUS

The Giganotosaurus discovered in Argentina in 1993 has a larger skull and thigh bone than the biggest T. rex!

Big appetite

It is no surprise to learn that these giant carnivores had an appetite to match their size. Discoveries of *titanosaurid* remains—big dinosaurs themselves—in *Giganotosaurus* territory suggest that even huge herbivores were a potential meal for this giant.

Fact File

How to say it JI-gah-no-tuh-SORE-us
Meaning of name Giant southern lizard
Family Allosauridae
Period Mid Cretaceous
Where found Argentina
Height 10 feet (3 meters)
Length 43 feet (13 meters)
Weight 6 tons (5,400 kilograms)
Food Meat
Special features Biggest carnivore of all?

SPINOSAURUS

This dinosaur might look a bit odd, but you wouldn't have wanted to say that to its face—this late Cretaceous predator was even longer than *Giganotosaurus*.

Sail

The most striking feature of *Spinosaurus* was the huge sail on its back. This wasn't for any kind of defensive purpose—a meat-eater like this had little to fear—instead, it was used to regulate the dinosaur's temperature. Blood was pumped around the sail, where it was either heated in the sun or cooled in the shade; this, in turn, controlled the temperature of *Spinosaurus*. Although sails were a relatively rare feature, they were found on other dinosaurs, as well as on reptiles such as *Dimetrodon*, which were around even earlier than the dinosaurs.

TRIASSIC   JURASSIC   CRETACEOUS

Fact File

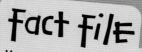

How to say it SPINE-oh-SORE-us
Meaning of name Thorn lizard
Family Spinosauridae
Period Late Cretaceous
Where found Egypt, Morocco
Height 16 feet 6 inches (5 meters)
Length 53 feet (16 meters)
Weight 4 tons (3,600 kilograms)
Food Meat
Special features Large sail

Something fishy

The best place to spot *Spinosaurus* was along the water's edge since it was a fish-eating dinosaur. The advantages of eating fish are obvious—because there were few dinosaurs with a taste for fish, *Spinosaurus* always had a big supply to hand.

Although Spinosaurus loved fish, when it fancied a change it would snap up anything else that came within reach.

BRACHIOSAURUS

One of the biggest, most famous dinosaurs of all time, *Brachiosaurus* was a true giant of the Jurassic world.

Going up

Besides its long neck, another contributing factor to the extreme height of *Brachiosaurus* was the fact that its front legs were considerably longer than its back ones. This gave *Brachiosaurus* an unusual upright stance and a marked advantage. As any giraffe knows, the youngest, juiciest shoots are at the top of a tree, and, if you're the tallest, you're the one who gets to eat them.

Fact File

How to say it BRAK-ee-oh-SORE-us
Meaning of name Arm lizard
Family Brachiosauridae
Period Late Jurassic
Where found Algeria, Portugal, Tanzania, USA
Height 53 feet (16 meters)
Length 99 feet (30 meters)
Weight 88 tons (80,000 kilograms)
Food Plants
Special features Extreme height

A Brachiosaurus's leg was around five times longer than that of an ostrich, the biggest bird around today.

TRIASSIC   JURASSIC   CRETACEOUS

Pumping

Paleontologists are puzzled by how *Brachiosaurus* managed to walk around without fainting: with a head so far away from its body, getting blood to the brain must have been really difficult. Did it perhaps have two hearts? Probably not, but this dinosaur must have had an extremely powerful heart to get the blood all the way up there. Unfortunately, we just don't know for sure.

8

DIPLODOCUS

One of the most famous dinosaurs of all was *Diplodocus*, a huge but gentle and relatively slender giant. It traveled in herds, constantly on the move to find new grazing areas.

Long neck and tail

The most obvious feature of *Diplodocus* was its extremely long neck and tail. Its neck was about 26 feet (8 meters) long, but its tiny head was less than 3 feet 3 inches (1 meter). The tail was as impressive as the neck and made an effective whiplike weapon for repelling predators.

Paleontologists believe that Diplodocus was partial to ferns in its diet.

Fact File

How to say it di-PLO-do-KUS
Meaning of name Double beam
Family Diplodocidae
Period Late Jurassic
Where found USA
Height 16 feet (5 meters)
Length 89 feet (27 meters)
Weight 12 tons (11,000 kilograms)
Food Plants
Special features Long neck and tail

TRIASSIC   JURASSIC   CRETACEOUS

Ground feeder

Not all long-necked dinosaurs ate
leaves from the treetops, and
Diplodocus was a good example
of this. Its front legs were shorter
than its hind legs, so its neck
naturally pointed down rather
than up. The extreme length of
its neck allowed *Diplodocus* to
graze over a large area of ground
without having to move.

SEISMOSAURUS

Seismosaurus is a real record breaker, since many paleontologists believe it was the longest of all dinosaurs. It would have been a great specimen to observe, as long as you kept clear of that vicious tail.

Short legs

Seismosaurus might have been the longest dinosaur, but it wasn't the tallest by any means, because of its relatively short legs. These little legs (and the front ones are shorter than the back) might have helped to make *Seismosaurus* a little more stable—a good thing, since you wouldn't want one of these creatures falling on you.

Longest of all

At around 110 feet (40 meters), *Seismosaurus* was a very long dinosaur indeed, and the longest animal ever to have lived. When a herd of these giants were on the move, you could guarantee that the front of the group would be far ahead of the back.

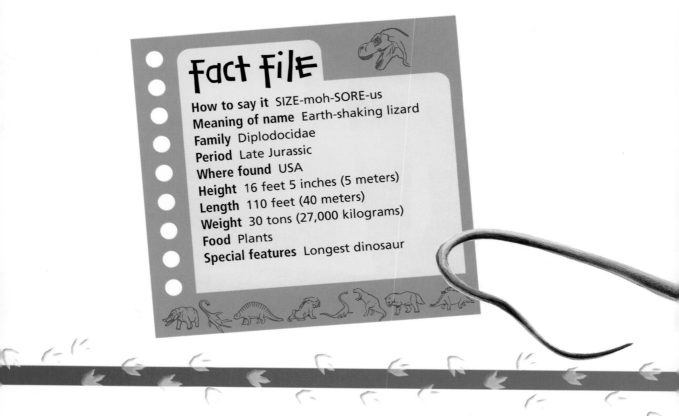

Fact File

How to say it SIZE-moh-SORE-us
Meaning of name Earth-shaking lizard
Family Diplodocidae
Period Late Jurassic
Where found USA
Height 16 feet 5 inches (5 meters)
Length 110 feet (40 meters)
Weight 30 tons (27,000 kilograms)
Food Plants
Special features Longest dinosaur

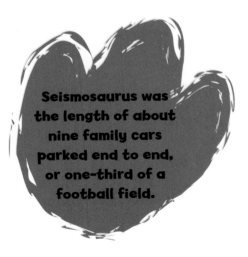

Too big for forests

Like its cousin, *Diplodocus*, *Seismosaurus* had a long neck. In addition to allowing it to graze over a large area without moving, this also allowed the dinosaur to nose around places its bulky body prevented it from going, such as in between trees.

Peg-like teeth

Seismosaurus had peg-like teeth, like *Diplodocus*. These were ideal for stripping vegetation from trees or low-lying shrubs but they were not so good for chewing up food. As a result, *Seismosaurus* swallowed the leaves and stems more or less whole.

Seismosaurus was the length of about nine family cars parked end to end, or one-third of a football field.

TRIASSIC   JURASSIC   CRETACEOUS

APATOSAURUS

Apatosaurus was a huge sauropod, one of the biggest types of dinosaur. Its sheer size was enough to put off most predators, and its long neck was excellent for grazing plants and leaves beyond the reach of other herbivores.

Two into one

For many years, the most complete *Apatosaurus* skeleton ever found was thought to belong to an entirely different dinosaur—*Brontosaurus*, which became one of the best-known dinosaurs. However, it was finally proved that *Brontosaurus* and *Apatosaurus* were the same creature.

Water-dweller?

The nostrils of *Apatosaurus* were located on the top of its head. In the past, some people believed it might have lived in water, like a hippopotamus. This seemed to make sense—the water would help support the dinosaur's massive body and *Apatosaurus* could breathe by sticking the top of its head out of the water. However, we now have firm evidence that this dinosaur was a land-dweller.

Fact File

How to say it a-PAT-oh-SORE-us
Meaning of name Deceptive lizard
Family Diplodocidae
Period Late Jurassic
Where found USA
Height 13 feet (4 meters)
Length 69 feet (21 meters)
Weight 33 tons (30,000 kilograms)
Food Plants
Special features Enormous size

Brontosaurus went on show at the American Museum of Natural History in 1905, the first sauropod to be exhibited.

TRIASSIC   JURASSIC   CRETACEOUS

QUAESITOSAURUS

This long-necked sauropod moved in herds across Mongolia. Like its cousin, *Diplodocus*, it had a whiplike tail that it used as a weapon against predators.

Massive muncher

Quaesitosaurus, like all the large sauropods, had to consume a huge amount of food every day just to keep going. For a big dinosaur, it only had a little mouth, so those jaws worked hard every day, especially since leaves were not always the most nutritious of foods. These dinosaurs spent most of their time eating.

Stomach stones

Many plant-eating dinosaurs— *Quaesitosaurus* included—carried gastroliths in their stomachs. These are stones that the dinosaur swallowed to help grind up the food inside its stomach. Some birds, such as chickens, do this too.

Quaesitosaurus had a big ear opening and is thought to have had good hearing.

TRIASSIC	JURASSIC	CRETACEOUS

Fact File

How to say it kway-zee-tuh-SORE-us
Meaning of name Abnormal lizard
Family Diplodocidae
Period Late Cretaceous
Where found Mongolia
Height 25 feet (7.6 meters)
Length 66 feet (20 meters)
Weight Not known
Food Plants
Special features Whiplike tail

Picture credits

© Shutterstock: front and back cover.

© De Agostini Picture Library: pages 2–9; 14–15

© Miles Kelly Publishing Ltd: pages 10–11

© Highlights for Children, Inc: pages 12–13

This edition published in 2012 by Arcturus Publishing Limited
26/27 Bickels Yard, 151–153 Bermondsey Street,
London SE1 3HA

Copyright © 2012 Arcturus Publishing Limited

ISBN: 978-1-84858-672-7
CH002334US
Supplier 15, Date 0312, Print run 1746

Printed in China